WHAT PEOPLE ARE SAYING ABOUT

THE URBAN OVATE

A clear, sensible and intensely personal book, based on extensive individual experience.
Professor Ronald Hutton, author of *Pagan Britain, The Druids* and *Blood and Mistletoe: The History of the Druids in Britain.*

The work of the Ovate is inward looking in nature, and so is easily available wherever you live. This makes it ideal for urban Pagans. Brendan Howlin explores this aspect of the Druid path with reference to pop culture and personal experience. It is a very readable introduction that should help people decide whether this is a path they want to travel further along.
Nimue Brown, author of *Pagan Portals: Spirituality without Structure, Druidry and Meditation* and *Pagan Planet: Being, Believing and Belonging in the 21st Century*

A cheerful introduction to what might be termed 'Psychological Druidry' that addresses the intermediate or 'Ovate' phase of a Druid's training. This book is partly a memoir of the Druid author himself, and partly a spiritual guide with searching questions that lead to the reader's greater self-awareness. A good book for the aspiring Druidic seeker.
Ellen Evert Hopman, author of *A Druid's Herbal of Sacred Tree Medicine* and *A Legacy of Druids – Conversations with Druid Leaders in Britain, the USA and Canada*

T0167904

Pagan Portals
The Urban Ovate
The Handbook of Psychological Druidry

Pagan Portals
The Urban Ovate
The Handbook of Psychological Druidry

Brendan Howlin

MOON
BOOKS

Winchester, UK
Washington, USA

First published by Moon Books, 2016
Moon Books is an imprint of John Hunt Publishing Ltd., Laurel House, Station Approach,
Alresford, Hants, SO24 9JH, UK
office1@jhpbooks.net
www.johnhuntpublishing.com
www.moon-books.net

For distributor details and how to order please visit the 'Ordering' section on our website.

ISBN: 978 1 78099 897 8
978 1 78099 898 5 (ebook)
Library of Congress Control Number: 2016934236

A CIP catalogue record for this book is available from the British Library.

Design: Stuart Davies

Printed and bound by CPI Group (UK) Ltd, Croydon, CR0 4YY, UK

We operate a distinctive and ethical publishing philosophy in all
areas of our business, from our global network of authors to
production and worldwide distribution.

Contents

For my muse as always, you know who you are.

Acknowledgements

Once again there are numerous people who deserve a mention and without whom this would be a much poorer book. I would particularly like to acknowledge Judy Peters, who believed from the beginning. My thanks go to Scott Turner and Sub Reddy for their valuable discussions on current female archetypes. For someone like me who doesn't watch much television it was invaluable. I would like to acknowledge the support from my fellow Moon Books authors, it is more like an extended family than a business. As always my OBOD tutees have really written this themselves over the years. I was overwhelmed at the support shown for the *Handbook of Urban Druidry* from people from all walks of life and the nice comments that people sent me. The best comment was from Caroline Staines, an ex-tutee, who said, on hearing me interviewed on Heretic Radio, that she was surprised at how I sounded after all the years of corresponding by letter…sorry for being a disappointment. However, she did say she was looking forward to my new book aimed at 'spiky Ovates' so here it is! People who read the drafts of this book for me said that it is not as witty as the first and that is the case, as Ovate is a darker, deeper and less amusing stage, but a highly necessary stage nonetheless. As before please send me your comments at the handbook of Urban Druidry Facebook page or website or email me on urbandruid1@gmail.com.

Continuing the Journey

I am assuming that you have read *The Handbook of Urban Druidry* and have practised some of the exercises outlined in there, so you are well on your way to becoming an Urban Druid. When you are writing a novel (which I am sure most of you are!) you are advised to describe scenes by using all of the senses, in order to draw your reader in and make your scenes believable. So you are advised to describe what the character sees, hears, touches, smells and sometimes tastes. It seems pretty obvious to me that we should be doing the same things with life in order to make it 'real'. If you have taken to heart my exhortations in the previous book, you should now be able to stand in your local patch of greenery and see the trees and flowers, hear the birds singing, smell the earth (especially if it is wet, which if you are in the UK will be most of the time!) and perhaps touch a leaf. Taste is always the most difficult one to express openly, but anyway, you will be present in the here and now. To take another example, I love to lie in bed at night listening to the rain and the wind. I like to hear the rain, but also feel warm and comfortable in my bed. There is a delicious melancholy to it that is worth savouring and I find it really peaceful. I don't find it quite so pleasant if I have to go to work in it the next day of course, but at least I have been present for the short time that I experienced it at night.

So now that you have learned to be present in your life, what next I hear you ask? How can I enrich my life even more than I have already? Basically, the first stage of Druid training is called the Bardic level, which is about what I described in the previous paragraph and also about freeing your imagination and creativity. Clearly this is an ongoing process, so don't worry if you feel that you are not exactly firing on all of these cylinders at once yet. The next step on the Druid journey is called the Ovate stage, which is basically finding out what makes you do the things you do. This sounds utterly trivial, but is one of the most difficult things to come to terms with in life.

When I mentioned this to one of my brothers he said that what makes you do the things that you do are beer and food! However, life is never that simple. As an example, we all remember moments when we have thought, 'Why did I do that?' So, if you are aware of what makes you do things you can take steps to only do those things that you want. We are also all subject to various levels of conditioning, some of which are very useful as they enable us to function in society, but there are some that are not. You have probably all met people who say, for example, that they want to lose weight but can't. This is, in the majority of cases, because their conscious self and their subconscious don't agree, as I mentioned in the previous book. Therefore, if you can find out what drives you then you can become a whole person, who is driven by your own will and not by anyone else's! These influencing factors can be broken down into several influences, which in Druidry we call spirits of something. This can be hard to understand, but I can make it simpler. What makes you do what you do is influenced by:

- Your culture
- Your genetic inheritance
- Your local environment
- The pressures of expectations
- Where you are in history

Out of these influences, your culture is the easiest to understand. Please note that I am not recommending or criticising anyone's culture. Everyone is different and it is not for me to say whether you should do one thing or another; the point of this exercise is to find out if you are doing things because they are expected of you and not because you really want to. I know lots of examples of this process of discovery that have happened to my tutees over the years, but I am forbidden by ethics and my oath of secrecy to reveal them, so what I am going to do is use myself as an example. This is not because I am a narcissist (well not much), but I have given myself permission to talk about myself. It is highly likely that my example won't resonate strongly with your life, as we will probably differ in age, sex and background, but I hope that it will make you think about your own influences. As an added aside, everyone likes snooping into other people's lives (after all what is Facebook for?), so you may also find it entertaining.

Your Culture

I am from an Irish culture, in that both of my parents were Irish. Despite the fact that I was born and raised in London, this is still the culture I grew up in. By this I mean that I share the characteristics of my race. Irish people like to have the 'craic', which is singing, dancing and drinking. We are sentimental and like slushy songs. We have been described as having an hysterical temperament, in that we are easily upset, don't control our emotions well and tend to bear grudges when we are crossed. If you want evidence of the Irish ability to hold grudges you just have to look at the Northern Irish problem. On the positive side we are happy, like jokes (even against ourselves) and like to talk socially.

Our love of drinking can be a bad thing, in that we get drunk easily, but don't stop when we have had enough and this can lead to fights or violence. In fact when I first went out with my future wife, we went to a pub and she jokingly asked me when I was going to start fighting! Fortunately I am also a coward and don't like violence. This shows that you don't have to subscribe wholly (or even partially) to the racial stereotype of your culture and a lot of people don't, but it is important to be aware of the cultural pressures that you are under, especially if you are unaware that you have any.

Incidentally, a lot of people don't like these cultural stereotypes and this resulted in my first rejection of an article for Touchstone, the Druid journal. I wrote an article about the genome of a typical Irishman being sequenced and thought I would make it more interesting by pointing out that the genes for drunkenness weren't located. Penny, the editor, rightly rejected the article by pointing out that many people put aside their sense of humour when they put on the Druid robe.

Another characteristic of Irish people is that they love to

argue, frequently taking a stance that they don't believe in just for the sake of arguing. Yet another aspect of the Irish is that they love to tell stories, but a story is best told with a little embellishment for effect. I was flabbergasted to find out that my wife (who comes from a staunch Presbyterian background) calls this lying, but everyone does this when they tell stories don't they? So this is a trivial example of cultural heritages leading to misunderstanding.

If you are not familiar with the approach of discovering your cultural heritage, it can be somewhat confusing. So think about your culture and see if it has any influences on you or not. You might be surprised by what you find. When you have thought about this decide whether the cultural behaviour you display is actually appropriate to you now. You may find that it is, in which case that is great, but if it is not then why continue to do it? When you have done this you have completed the first stage in finding out what moves you.

1) What is your culture?
2) What characterises your culture?
3) Do you display any of these characteristics?

Your Genetic Inheritance

This can be a troublesome area as it smacks of eugenics and racial profiling, but it doesn't really. In fact, if you are European, your genetic inheritance shows that we are actually all brothers and sisters. This also applies to most Americans as well because many Americans originated in Europe. A guy called Professor Bryan Sykes wrote a book in 2001 called *The Seven Daughters of Eve* in which he postulated that all people in Europe were descended from just seven women, and 40 per cent of the people in Europe from just one. As many of the people in North America are also derived from European peoples, it is probably true for them too. This was a startling revelation at the time and caused a lot of excitement.

Subsequently there is evidence for another Scandinavian family and some dispute as to whether there should be 12 families, but the point still stands. We are all descended from a very small group of people.

Obviously there were more than seven women alive at the time that each of the 'Daughters of Eve' lived, but the theory goes that the others didn't give rise to descendants that crossed the centuries or only had sons. Yes, that's right only sons; the genetic material that they are tracking is only passed through the matrilineal line, so boys don't count. These women didn't live at the same time, but very roughly date back to about 50,000 years ago. I was talking about this in a lecture a few years ago and a student came up to me afterwards. I was astonished that a student had actually listened to what I was saying and had something to contribute! Anyway, he was Indonesian and pointed out that there was a super volcano that exploded in Indonesia 50,000 years ago and this may have nearly wiped out the human race. So it was entirely feasible that we could be descended from a small population of people.

In case you are interested, the DNA they are tracking is in the mitochondria of your cells (these provide the energy for your cells), which are only passed on by the female egg cells. They are not passed from the sperm, so only the female contributes to the transfer of this information. As you have probably also realised, the reason that female inheritance can be tracked back so far is because for a lot of history the fate of women was to wait for the next barbarian to knock down their door and slaughter their husband and children. Invaders rarely kill the women, and as women therefore didn't move around very much they have deep ancestral connections to where they live. A good example of this is in Neil Oliver's book on the Vikings (not Celtic so not in the reading list, sorry Neil) where he states that the women in the Shetland Islands can be tracked back for 12,000 years or so and all of the men are genetically Vikings.

If you would like to know which tribe you belong to you can get a determination from www.oxfordancestors.com for about £200. I am not an advocate for any commercial organisation so this is only given for information. They used to do it by sending you a scraper that you used to collect some cells from the inside of your cheek. I remember doing this with 14 students in a forensics practical once and only three of them turned out to be human, i.e. only three had any DNA at all, so you need to scrape thoroughly.

Your genetic inheritance is, of course, also related to the Human Genome Project, which promised so much and gave us an exciting race between the academics and the commercial company that tried to be the first to do it. Yes, maybe I should get out more. Anyway, one of the main conclusions of this was a somewhat surprising one, but important for Druidry. The DNA in your cells codes for the proteins that make up your body, so one would expect that in a complex creature like a human there would be lots of genes coding for a wide variety of proteins. This turned out not to be the case, the human genome codes for only about 20,000 proteins. This number of genes is not significantly more than those of a fruit fly. This is a sobering thought, that you are no more complex from this point of view than a tiny black fly! So there is no evidence in the genome for our complexity. This is an area of hot dispute at the moment, but from a Druidry point of view it highlights the commonality of all life on earth, which is something that many Druids believe in.

Incidentally, as you have probably realised, there is currently nothing in your DNA to account for consciousness. So the current theory is that consciousness comes from outside...hmmm, what does that sound like? Incidentally, I love telling students that they are no more complex genetically than a fruit fly, but that is just my perverse sense of humour.

So if your genetic inheritance only demonstrates the fact that we are not different, what is the point? The point is that there are certain genetic peculiarities that characterise certain peoples. The most well known of these is the lack of the gene for the protein alcohol dehydrogenase in Chinese people. This protein serves to detoxify alcohol when it is taken into the human body. Chinese people in general tend to lack this protein and as a result can't drink much alcohol. So knowing this, if you are Chinese, drinking may not be a big part of your life. Clearly this is a trivial example, but the point stands. Incidentally it is also possible to induce the ability to drink alcohol if you are Chinese by drinking and being sick until you can take it. I know of at least one young person who did this because she wanted to associate with her friends who were not of Chinese origin and did drink. However, as you can see, it is not recommended.

Another well-known example is sickle cell anaemia in people of Afro-Caribbean origin, where the sickle blood cells confer immunity to malaria, which is why it evolved, but it also confers a disadvantage in the oxygen carrying capacity of the blood. These effects of single mutations also go by the name of epigenetics or personalised medicine these days, so is becoming more important and may revolutionise the way we are all treated by medicine in the future.

Recently the complete genome of a representative Irishman was sequenced (if there is any such thing as a representative Irishman!). The results from this study showed that the Irish are genetically distinct from the rest of Europe and they may have identified markers that they can use to define 'Irishness'. This is the good news and is perhaps not unexpected as the Irish are a race that was isolated at the edge of Western Europe and the population is, to say the least, a little 'inbred'. Obviously the Irish are also over-represented in the populations of North America and Australia. The bad news is that they have also isolated markers with the potential for chronic liver disease and inflammatory bowel disease. This just means that Irish people are susceptible to these illnesses, not that every Irish person will get them.

Scientists who know about DNA speak of two influences, the genetic one and the influence of the environment (which is called phenotypic). What this means is that we are not slaves to our genetic makeup and can be different depending on what we are exposed to. To take this analogy further, you share a great deal of your DNA with your brothers and sisters, but you may look and behave completely differently. This phenotypic difference comes into the next influence.

1) What is your genetic inheritance?
2) What traits characterise your genetic inheritance?
3) Do you display any of these traits?

Your Local Environment

How you grew up affects how you do things. When I was growing up in the mid-1960s and early 1970s in the East End of London, things were very different to how they are now. For a start personal computers didn't exist, there was no internet, televisions were black-and-white and music was played by putting circular black plastic discs called records on to a record player. Consequently we spent most of our time outside playing in the street. The lamp post outside my house was the congregation point for the neighbourhood kids and there was a kind of initiation that involved having to climb the lamp post and swing from the parallel bar on it that was about six feet from the ground. Very few people had cars in those days so we had to only rarely interrupt our games to let a car go past. I remember my mother coming out to complain when we kicked our football against the wall opposite, which was the wall of the convent. My mother was afraid that we would disturb the nuns! We even had our own Tardis (if you have watched the BBC TV programme Doctor Who, this will mean something to you). The police box was on the corner of the road, so formed a centrepiece of our games. I can't remember if anyone actually went inside it. In fact I think no one did because we were all afraid of the police. This was despite the fact that there was a kindly old sergeant on television on Saturday nights in Dixon of Dock Green. Most houses in those days had coal fires, there was no central heating and in the winter we had to wait for my mother to get up first and light the fire before venturing out of bed ourselves. We were adept at getting dressed without getting out of bed because it was so cold.

Everyone went to Saturday morning pictures at the local cinema where we were encouraged to sing along to the Lambeth Walk by watching a little dot go over the words on the screen at the correct pace. We saw serials such as Flash Gordon, Superman or Batman and a main film, which was some worthy offering from the British Film Institute encouraging us to be tolerant of others, for example. When I say everyone went, I do mean everyone, even those who couldn't pay. The first few kids in would open the fire escape doors for everyone else. We couldn't work out why they didn't lock them, but as they were fire escapes I guess they couldn't. I also wondered why the cinema owners couldn't work out that there were twice as many people in the cinema as they had sold tickets to.

Going to fetch the coal was a regular event, which involved going down the stairs into the coal cellar (which all houses had). My brother never tired of turning off the light and locking the cellar door when you went down. You had then to bang on the door until help came or climb out of the coal hole cover into the porch of the house and knock on the front door to get back in again. Children weren't trusted with keys then.

As there were six children in my family, no one had their own room and sharing things was a way of life. It was also a way of life to steal someone's chair if they got up to do something or go to the toilet, so there was a constant shuffling back and forth all evening as we competed for the best chairs in the living room. This was a source of great embarrassment to my mother when the local Catholic priest was visiting one day and got up to visit the toilet and someone stole his chair. Naturally the priest came from a large family himself and was quite happy to get involved in the rough and tumble of family life, but my mother was still mortified.

When my future wife first came to tea with my family, she waited politely to be offered food, but to no avail, as my brothers and I just helped ourselves to everything. Maybe this is why I eat so fast, though my wife reminds me that no one is going to steal the food off my plate now!

There wasn't a lot of contact with green space in the East End of London. The local park was policed by park keepers whose sole function seemed to be to keep kids out of the park. However, like most Irish families at that time, we spent our entire summer holidays in Ireland on my aunt's farm. So we had every opportunity to get out in the rain and be free. As an aside, I experienced the evolution of farming from horses through threshing machines to tractors, to combine harvesters, but that is a story for another time (can't resist the Bardic urge).

I was sitting in a course on unconscious bias a while ago and realised that my upbringing in the East End of London meant that I wasn't in the least bit unconsciously biased, in fact I was pretty much consciously biased about everyone and everything! As an aside I also discovered that if I spoke as I should, meaning with a strong cockney accent, then only 11 per cent of people in the UK would think that I was intelligent! There were three of us in the course who were university professors and the other two professors were from Liverpool and Somerset. All three of these accents have the lowest percentage of perception of intelligence in the UK. Suffice it to say that none of us actually spoke with our native accents, having all adopted an indeterminate posh version as a form of unconscious intellectual camouflage. So, if you thought that Lerner and Loewe's My Fair Lady (Shaw's Pygmalion if you are a theatre-goer) was only relevant to the Victorian age in the UK then think again. This is a classic example of an assumption that you are consciously unaware of, leading to treating someone differently.

As I have travelled through life and become conscious of the spiritual path I am travelling I have noted that life has presented me with opportunities to confront all of my biases. As a first generation Irish Catholic growing up in London, I hadn't met a Protestant until I was 18. I didn't quite expect them to have horns and a tail, but almost. I remember a progressive teacher in school asking us to write down as many Protestant factions as we could and we all gaped in astonishment, there were Catholics and

Protestants – that was it! One of my Greek tutees once told me about the priest in his school expostulating about the bloody Catholics, the bloody Protestants and the lovely Greek Orthodox. Anyway, suffice to say that when I actually met Protestants at university they turned out to be perfectly nice people.

As I continued my journey I was offered the opportunity to remove my biases against women, gays and so on. Strangely enough, I wasn't biased against black people because the next door neighbours were from the Caribbean and they were really nice people and we played together in the street. My wife likes to gently chide me about my prejudices and recently she pointed out to me that I was confronting my last bias, having found out that one of my Druid tutees was a policeman, who invited me to have coffee with him. He is also a perfectly nice person, which is a great change in my attitude from my childhood, where we hated the police. In fact the police had a good reason to dislike us, as it was the Irish who were bombing London at the time and it is easy to spot an Irishman. Actually I have become more Irish-looking as I got older and this can actually be useful because in a big customs queue in Boston airport once, the official spotted me and said, 'You can come through Sir!' having spotted a fellow countryman!

Racial bias can be a frightening thing; I was exposed to it on an underground train in London in my youth. I was going to work in the morning and the train had stopped at Stepney Green tube station. A man got on and started shouting at me accusing me of being Jewish. I was very young and didn't know what to do, so I tried to get off, but he followed me until he felt he had harassed me enough and left me alone. I thought about telling him that I was not Jewish, but Catholic, and that curly black hair and large noses are common between the two races, but realised that it would make no difference.

Later on in life, I went Golem hunting in Prague and was standing in the Old Jewish cemetery at Rabbi Loew's grave and expostulating to my companions about the Golem, when a Jewish girl came up and wanted to know what was going on, so I ended up teaching her about her own traditions. This rather backfired because two Canadian ladies came up afterwards and said, 'This must make you very sad.' However, they meant well, so I didn't bother to correct them, but I made the mistake of thinking they were Americans, which is probably also an insult.

Incidentally I wasn't actually hunting Golems, but just wanted to see the places made famous in the stories (see the reading list if you don't know these stories) and wanted to see where Dr John Dee, the famous Elizabethan magician, had been when he was in Prague. *The Angel of the West Window* by Gustav Meyrink covers Dee's time in Prague very nicely. Incidentally, if you think you don't know the story of the Golem, think again. Superman was born out of the same mythology and shares some common features with the Golem. The Golem was an automaton and Superman displays some automaton-like behaviour. The Golem was designed to protect the inhabitants of the Ghetto in Prague whereas Superman protects the world. The Golem could be switched off when not needed and so can Superman when he is exposed to green kryptonite. The Golem also became unpredictable, just like Superman when he is exposed to red kryptonite.

So this is a classic case of the myths of a people being updated for the modern age. We will come back to this in the discussion on Gods and Goddesses as Superman is also an incarnation of the Sun God. Of course Prague is also a nice place to visit, an unsolicited plug for the Prague Tourist Board!

The moral of this is look closely at your prejudices and see which ones you have, even if you are currently unaware that you have them. You will then be able to confront them and if you move beyond them you will be a much better person.

The concept of privacy was virtually unknown to me as a child. There was very little that was actually owned by me. In fact, most of my clothes were hand-me-downs from my older brother or cousins. To this day I cannot bear wearing old clothes; everything I have has been bought new by me. So this expectation that I will share everything, am used to having a lot of people around, like being outside doing things and don't often listen to music are all part of my upbringing.

What I needed to ask myself when I did the Ovate course was, are those things still a part of me or are they no longer appropriate? Initially, I couldn't stand being alone, but as time went on I got more used to it and it is now a big part of my life. However, there are some people who haven't changed that much from when they were kids and you have to ask why not?

1) What is your local environment?
2) What have you picked up from it?
3) Are these behaviours still appropriate?

The Pressures of Expectations

This is a thorny one, as some people don't accept that they are subject to the pressures of expectations at all. I once tried to explain to someone that there are certain expectations that we have about the role of a wife, which we might not be aware of but that we have anyway. I was told that he certainly didn't have them and would never treat his wife that way, so happy woman I say!

However, if you are more average than this there is every chance that you do. These pressures are insidious as most people don't know that they have them, so they are difficult to spot. To make it clearer, there are roles traditionally assigned to a husband or wife that we often assume they will do without actually asking them if it is appropriate to cast them in that role. Traditionally, the wife in western society did the cooking, cleaning, ironing, looked after the kids and dealt with social interactions with her own and her husband's family. The husband was the main breadwinner, dealt with the bills, fixed the car and did any maintenance that was required around the house. I know you will say that we have moved on a great deal from these stereotypes and if so then great, but have we really?

Many women work these days and some earn more than their husbands. Many men help with the kids and even do some housework, but how equal are things really? All I'm really asking is to become aware of the expectations that go with the roles and see if they apply to you.

I understand that Buddhists believe that unhappiness is caused by expectations; the corollary of this is that if you expect nothing then you won't be disappointed, but that is a hard way to live. Having said that, much of our joy in life is marred by expectations and in some ways it is harder than ever in our modern world. In medieval times your role in life was fixed from birth, if you were born to a blacksmith then a blacksmith you would be, or if you were the son of a lord then the new lord you would be. The concept of social mobility just didn't exist; everyone knew their place and kept to it. Stress in the modern sense just didn't exist; this modern stress is caused to a great extent by expectations.

In our modern world, it is possible to be anything and this has raised expectations to unsustainable levels. If it is possible to be just about anything then why aren't you? What is holding you back? Again as a corollary if you haven't become president of your corporation aren't you a failure? The secular world that we live in these days makes things worse; if money is your only God and you don't have it then you have failed. Also if you only have one life and you haven't succeeded then you are going to be extremely stressed.

I don't want to pontificate on whether we have more than one life (most unusual for me!), as many Druids believe in metempsychosis, which means reincarnation into another body after you die. In practice, if you believe in metempsychosis or not, it doesn't make much difference in the here and now, the only practical benefit of this belief is that it reduces stress now, as you can do better next time round. The main foundation of this belief is that the essential you gets transferred to the new body, but the new ego (or you) doesn't remember being someone else, so effectively it doesn't make a lot of difference. I believe that in Celtic times, this belief was so strong that you could arrange to pay debts back next time round, which had an obvious financial benefit for you. Unfortunately, it would also have a somewhat negative effect on whoever you were judged to have reincarnated as.

In the example I was just talking about before I digressed into the ego and reincarnation, i.e. the cultural experience, we also accepted the expectations of the time. Mothers were expected to exist just to tell you off about things, fathers were more or less absent (at least in their interactions with kids). Kids were

17

expected to make their own amusements and not to bother the adults. The modern concept of a partnership between kids and parents just didn't exist. In fact, in most of the novels we read that were written some time ago, the parents were got out of the way quickly at the start of the story because everyone knew that you couldn't have any fun if there were parents around. Nowadays, parents take their kids to rugby, extra classes, drama, etc and 'helicopter' around preventing their kids from showing any initiative or imagination of their own; the result is kids being unable to cope with any kind of stress. If asked, the parents would say that they are helping their kids to become accomplished and competitive, but it does seem like it is having the reverse effect.

This is extremely unfortunate because the world hasn't got less stressful and people need to be able to cope with more rather than less stress. So again, take time to review the expectations that you are operating under and see if they are actually appropriate to your life now.

The great herbalist Dr Richard Schulze, in his Healing the Incurables programme, goes around the houses of terminally ill people touching objects to see if he gets a reaction. One good example was someone's framed law certificate. This person's parents really wanted her to be a lawyer, so like a good child she complied. She really didn't want to fulfil that role, so the framed law certificate was actually toxic to her! I'm not saying that things like this are operating in your life, but it just goes to show how we can buy into things that really are not what we want, just to please others. Ultimately you have to please yourself and I don't mean you have to be dreadfully selfish and self-centred, but you must be happy with who you are and what you are doing.

1) What expectations are operative in your life?
2) Are they appropriate to you now?
3) What can you let go of to make your life easier?

The Ancestors

If I was to choose one thing that causes the most problems with tutoring the Druid course, I would choose this. Why, you might ask, because they are dead and gone aren't they? What power do they have over your life now? You might be surprised with the answer because the problem with the ancestors starts right at home. We have sort of touched on this already, but it is very succinctly summed up by the poet Philip Larkin in his poem 'This be the Verse', which I won't reproduce here for two reasons, one it is copyright and secondly it contains the odd rude word. If you haven't read it then I suggest you look it up, if you have then you will know that it is about parents. You would be surprised (or maybe not) by the number of people who have issues with their parents. In fact, I know of one case where the tutee literally ran away rather than face the issues and travelled around the world for eight years before returning home and facing them.

If you are a parent yourself you might take exception to this because in the majority of cases you are just trying to do your best, but that is the point; while trying to do your best you end up causing problems for your offspring to a greater or lesser extent. This is of course true for parents who are trying to help, but there are also those who are not helpful or downright damaging. The key is the bit about trying to do their best.

Parents are not supreme gurus, they don't know how to raise children any more than anyone else does and from time to time they make mistakes. As I said the key is to acknowledge that they may have made mistakes and then find in your heart some modicum of sympathy and understanding for them.

This is part of the ancestors section because many women have noticed that you turn into your mother when you have kids yourself. I know of one woman who was determined not to be

19

like her mother and knew she had failed when she found herself saying, 'Because I told you so!'

This forgiveness and acceptance is even possible with the extreme cases of parenting, as myself and a Druid friend both had schizophrenic fathers and we have managed to forgive them to some extent.

Once you have dealt with your immediate parents, you can turn your attention to earlier ancestors. In many cases this gets easier as a lot of people get on quite well with their grannies and granddads. Further back there may be problems lurking in the wings, the most common one being family expectations. For example, if you come from a military family and have no interest in a military career yourself, you can feel like a failure. I am reminded of the poet John Betjeman who was expected to inherit the family business and just wanted to write poetry instead.

So have a look and see what kind of a family you come from and see if you are representative of it. There is a vast array of ways in which you can search your family history now, online or not and there are even magazines devoted to it. If you get into it, it can provide an interesting hobby and you will also avoid the extremely common problem of getting interested in this just when those who can tell you about it have departed this plane.

It is inevitable that we will come to past life regression here. I haven't tried this myself so speak from pure bias and prejudice (yes, another one!). I have heard that many find this quite useful; my scepticism is based on the fact that many people who I have talked to about this seem to have been Cleopatra or Napoleon or someone equally historically famous in their previous lives. It seems to me that the chances are that the vast majority of people who have lived on this earth were probably nameless peasants who lived a brief life of penury and struggle before moving on at an early age. They would not have been famous people. Coupled to this is the ability of the subconscious mind to pick up things that you don't consciously know and the marvellous ability (which if you have read book 1, you will have trained) of the mind to imagine and invent things. These things combined could lead to the confusion of reality with fiction; in short making things up. This could be useful if your subconscious wants to tell you a story that you can then interpret, but not if you are going to delude yourself. So, in summary, I would recommend that you stick to the facts and use them to build a picture of your ancestral heritage.

I tried this myself, in the spirit of not asking others to do things that I can't do myself, and used the public library's copy of Ancestry.co.uk. You can have one hour's free access to this in Guildford library. During my hour I found myself (not hard as I know most of the details about myself!), several brothers and sisters, my parents and made a start on my grandparents. As I know almost nothing about my paternal grandfather, apart from the fact that I think his name was William, I did quite well. One of the William Howlins that I found even got married in Wexford (where my parents come from) to a woman called Mary (which I think was my paternal grandmother's name). Unfortunately this Mary's second name turned out to be Murphy, which caused a dead end, as you can readily imagine the sheer number of ladies with the name Mary Murphy in Ireland.

Interestingly I found a shipping list for a ship from South Africa to London in 1938 that carried my uncle Arthur to London, as I recognised the address he gave as the address of my paternal grandmother in Wexford. As I never met the man, because he died before I was born, I had no idea he had been to South Africa. So there you go – the results of an hour's search on the web.

It is entirely possible that you know a great deal more about your ancestors than I do and this is an area of great interest and fascination for you, if this is so, then that is great, because you have found one of those hobbies that I mentioned in book 1.

1) Do you know who your ancestors were?
2) Are you happy with your ancestral heritage?
3) Do you have issues with your parents? Can you forgive them?

Where are you in History?

This is also called the spirit of the age in Druidry and relates to the behaviour that is expected from you because of when you were born in a certain time. A lot of people might dispute that there is any such thing as a spirit of the age, but many if asked would describe the Victorian age in the United Kingdom as one of industry with hardworking men and women, all possessed of a certainty that British people were superior to all others and with a strong Christian faith.

Just by considering these qualities, one is immediately able to make a comparison to the spirit of the age in our own time. A few moments' speculation can give you an overview of modern Britain as post-industrial with people who don't want to work that hard with a post-imperialist guilt about British people and with a variety of faiths, but mostly none. You might well disagree with my reading here and you are most welcome to, if it makes you think I'm all for it. The same can be done for whichever country you live in. I won't attempt it because you could probably accuse me of bias and I would negate my earlier statements.

However, taking my reading as a working view, what does that mean for us now? The celebrity culture is one of these aspects, where people just want to be famous for being famous without actually having had to do anything. In the Victorian age, to be 'not the least of our merchant-princes', to quote Kipling, was one of the highest aspirations. As an example of this, I was being given a lift back from a hire car firm by a young lady driver once and she said that she had been talking to another young lady in a pub. This girl told her that she wanted to be a singer, so she asked her, 'Where do you sing?' It turned out that she didn't actually sing anywhere at all, but expected to be magically picked up as a singer by sitting around!

I have heard it said that in the UK, if you are a young person and you haven't, for some reason, been picked up to front a rock band by the time you are 18 then you might as well go to university. Admittedly I am not of this generation, but in my day we went to university because we wanted to do something that interested us and that we would be able to get a decent job in afterwards.

Perhaps the biggest difference between people now and in my youth is socialism. In my day if you weren't a socialist it was tantamount to saying that you were a child molester and my life could well be catalogued under the failure of the socialist dream. There was going to be a new world order where everyone would be equal, money and goods would be shared fairly and people would understand and care about each other. Yes, we actually believed this, but what we got was political correctness where it was forbidden to speak out against anything, a 'jobsworth' culture where people would only do what they felt like, and the death of religion bringing about the secular world we now inhabit. Those of you who have been staying awake will notice that I have already mentioned the secular world, so thank you for keeping up!

The socialist views that we held, we weren't aware that we had picked up because everyone around us thought and felt the same, or at least we thought they did. They were part of the cultural brainwashing that was the spirit of the age in the 1960s and 70s before Thatcherism swept it away in the 80s with the rise of Yuppies. This was followed by the blatant expediency of the Blair years, where it didn't matter what you said or believed as long as you benefitted personally from it and then we had the coalition, where we were all in it together and new austerity briefly evoked the 'make do and mend' of the war generations. In this phase, expediency reached its logical absurdity with the bankers bankrupting the country because they gambled with our money and lied about their losses.

So which spirit moves you? Recognising and acknowledging it is the first part of the battle because if you are moved by unconscious demands and beliefs you are not your own person. Of course the spirit of the age may not be a wholly negative thing; I read recently about a black American saying that white people have gotten nicer, so that is something really positive. Referring back to my discussion of prejudice earlier, it is fair to say that people these days generally know a lot more about other people's cultures and are much more accepting of them. The colour of someone's skin is hardly a matter of note at all among groups of young people in the UK. To really develop this theme would probably be a sociology PhD thesis so I'm not going to do that; it is not as if I am in the least bit qualified to do that anyway, but the important thing to note is that everything changes.

We assume (incorrectly) that things stand still around us, but the only thing that is constant is change. In the days of my parents' childhood, they travelled around by pony and trap, whereas children these days are accustomed to being driven everywhere by car. So if the world is changing around you, why can't you change too if you need to?

1) What characterises the spirit of your age?
2) Do you display these characteristics?
3) Are they appropriate to you now?

Death

Death is the only surety in life; it is the only thing we can actually be certain of, the one thing that we will all experience. We do not like to think about it in our modern life; we have removed it from our daily lives. The meat that we eat (if we do) is killed and processed away from our sight and delivered to us in carefully wrapped packages that bear little resemblance to the animal it once was. The death of people has also been sanitised; bodies are removed from our houses to mortuaries where they are disposed of by funeral companies without our involvement. In a lot of cases our involvement is only to appear for half an hour at the crematorium for a short service after which the body is cremated and we wait to receive the ashes.

It was not always so in our society and there is a valid argument in removing the dead from the living in our society when there are so many people, to avoid the risk of disease, etc. However, death is part of the Ovate experience, our own eventual and hopefully far-off death and the smaller deaths like the death of the old you. In the *Tibetan Book of the Dead* there is a realisation that death is constantly with us, as we move through life and die to our old ways.

The thought of our own mortality is a worrying one to us because we exist supreme in the knowledge that we are the only thing we really know and we cannot conceive of it ever being different. However, if we can look death in the face and accept that it must happen someday, we can stop worrying about it and get on with the process of enjoying what we have now. The present is all we ever have and it is our duty to experience and love every moment. OK, I know that there are stressful moments when we aren't enjoying it, but even these are part of life.

One of the most harrowing books I have ever read was written by an ex-tutee of mine. He is a mortuary technician in his 'real' life and describes the process of death in intimate detail. I recommend that people read this; it will upset you, but in the end you will be glad that you did. It is called *The Journey into Spirit: A Pagan's Perspective on Death, Dying, and Bereavement* by Kristoffer Hughes and aptly addresses this last taboo. It also has a glowing recommendation from me on the cover, so what more could you want?

Because of the importance and significance of death, this is why the tree of the Ovate is the yew. Yew trees are often associated with graveyards and were the first trees to emerge from the Ice Age. They are truly eternal trees, with new growth arising from the death of the original, where they spread out in a ring from the central trunk. We use the yew as a symbol both of death and life eternal because, as I explained before, the subconscious mind understands symbols better than direct speech and your subconscious can understand and work with symbols like this. This is one of the reasons that Druids use trees, obviously there are many others.

1) How do you view your own death?
2) Does it upset you?
3) Can you come to terms with it?

Healing and Herbalism

The word Ovate comes from 'vates', which means seer and is one of the grades of the Druids recognised by Tacitus in his book *Germanica*, which is supposed to be about the Germanic tribes, but he seemed to be a little confused by the natives! So the Ovate is associated with the healing and divinatory arts, which to bring it right up to date means healing yourself of your physical and mental problems. You need to do this so that you can visualise what the complete and new you is going to be and get out there and do it. Hence all the Druid concern with healing, herbalism and divination is directed to this end. However, I might be wrong here (as always you say!) as there seems to be a growing movement among Druids to stop working on themselves and step out into the light and get involved with external things like activism. Let us just sweep this under the carpet for the time being (thereby condemning to obscurity many people's deeply held beliefs and struggles) and just concentrate on ourselves.

Healing is important because if even a small part of you aches you are conscious of it all of the time. The English essayist William Hazlitt once said, 'The least pain in our little finger gives us more concern and uneasiness than the destruction of millions of our fellow beings.' He died in 1830, but unfortunately his comments are still very relevant today. Any sort of illness or pain naturally detracts from your enjoyment of life and your ability to move forward. So get yourself well first, which is easily said and extremely difficult to do. If you have been following my recommendations in the first book, you will have gone a large way towards this end anyway.

Herbalism can help with this and so can ibuprofen and paracetamol. I can attest to this after suffering with Reiter's syndrome for a year. If you don't know, Reiter's is reactive arthritis, where your body decides to attack your joints for a period of up to a year and then stops as mysteriously as it started. It seems to be a family trait (genetic inheritance) in my case as my brother also had it at the same time. Anyway, the point of this is that you need to take ibuprofen and paracetamol to deal with the pain and without painkillers you don't feel very spiritual at all. I have encountered many people who swear by flax seeds for curing arthritis and it seems to work really well for them. I personally feel the need for conventional medicine in a lot of cases, but as always find what works for you.

A gravel pit in Stanway near Colchester in Essex might not sound like the place for the most significant archaeological finding for Druidry, but it is. In this humble gravel pit a series of graves were found dating from 40-60BC. One of the graves contains the cremated remains of what might be the only formal burial of a Druid found in the UK. Among the grave goods were a set of divining rods, a copper saucepan and copper strainer, a fancy (for the time) imported pottery service, a set of surgical implements, a jet bead, an ornate brooch and a cloak.

In the pottery, traces of mugwort (Artemisia) were found and its pollen was found in the strainer, indicating the use of this herb for either divination or healing. The surgical implements included scalpels, forceps and a surgical saw. So this is actually the only direct evidence we have for the herbs that were sacred to the Druids and, what is more important, were actually used. There are many reports of seven sacred herbs of the Druids and if we look at the story of Diancecht (see Gods and Goddesses) there may have been 365 sacred herbs (unspecified), but there are no actual confirmed written sources except this story of Diancecht. However, if you would like to know about a modern view on resurrecting this herbal lore, I recommend that you read Ellen Evert Hopman's *A Druid's Herbal for the Sacred Earth Year*.

Therefore, from the Ovate point of view, mugwort is the herb. However, if you are pregnant or think you might be you must have no contact with mugwort as it has been used in the past for inducing abortions. Mugwort can be placed under your pillow at night (bearing in mind the caution above) to induce dreams and drunk as a tea to relax the nervous system and also to induce dreams. This is why it is known as the visionary herb. As a further caution, if you are allergic to members of the daisy family you should also not use mugwort. Having said all this it is possible to buy mugwort at herbal supply stores if you want to increase your psychic powers or even flavour your beer, which is why it is called mugwort! Giving credit to the opposition, Roman soldiers put mugwort into the soles of their sandals to reduce fatigue and as they could march 20 miles a day perhaps it worked.

1) Are you well?
2) What ails you?
3) What can you do about it now?

Love

Perhaps the biggest cultural expectation in western culture is romantic love. I have spent many an hour speculating on whether love actually exists or is the most effective imposed expectation of them all and you will probably be glad to hear that I believe in love. Love is what makes life worthwhile, it raises you up and makes you better than you would be otherwise, which is actually what all this writing is about. The cynical view of love is that it gets you away from the fear of dying alone. However, many ladies expect to meet the one who will love and adore them and fulfil them in every way, the classic knight in shining armour! However, many ladies would accept that there is more than one 'one', i.e. if the love of their life dies then they would entertain the possibility that there is another 'one' out there for them. Is this just an excuse to avoid loneliness or is this 'real'?

This relates to the spirit of the age because this is very much a 21st century thing. Some might argue that love comes from our earliest recorded writings and is not a facet of current expectations. If we look a bit further at this we can see that the spirit of the age is working in personal relationships. I am sure we can all point to instances where a lady friend has taken up with someone we consider to be an unsuitable match because she loves him. Later on the lady in question cleans him up, gets him into a suitable job, gets the house, gets the requisite number of kids and/or dog(s) and the couple are then respectable members of society. If you've ever seen the hit musical Guys and Dolls the ladies in this sing, 'You can't get alterations on a dress you haven't bought!' which just about sums it up. Incidentally if you haven't read the stories of Damon Runyon that the musical is based on please do, they are excellent.

However, to get back to the point, there are extreme expectations acting on married couples to conform and become respectable members of society. This pressure is enacted by parents, grandparents, siblings, friends, television and so on, and it is extremely difficult to escape this conditioning. If you are a young lady who doesn't want kids you will be subjected to almost unbelievable pressure to have them from those around you, but if you think logically about it there are more than enough people in the world already, so why do you want more? Of course if you actually want kids and this is your actual desire then fine, but if you are just conditioned to think that you want them then you are not being true to yourself. Of course there are gentlemen who believe the same as well, but they invariably don't have the pressure to have kids because they can't actually have them. I am reminded of an acquaintance who once said he had never experienced sexual discrimination, but then he wouldn't have because he is a man!

Men can believe in love as ardently as any woman, but social conditioning (yes, that again!) means that it is considered unmanly to express this desire in public. Men should concentrate on their careers, which always come first and the wife and family come second...or should they? It is still considered somewhat odd if a man stays at home to be a househusband while his wife goes out to work, but why not if it suits you? In fact love is the one thing that attracts most of our expectations and unhappiness so it's well worth sorting out how you feel about it rather than being its slave and dragged willy-nilly about by it (and we all know people who act like this don't we!). If you don't know what willy-nilly means then don't despair as we (OBOD tutors that is) discovered that Americans don't have the same catchphrases as us and we had to explain some English expressions to American tutors and vice versa. This ought to have been startlingly obvious, but is an excellent example of cultural conditioning, so for your information if you need it, willy-nilly means whether one likes it or not.

Incidentally, this is why the Ovate course is so hard because you have to question your every action and desire and decide if you are doing what you will or what someone else wills and that makes the whole difference.

1) Is love important to you?
2) Who do you love?
3) Do you love enough?

Dreams

Dreams and divination are a large part of most Ovate courses because, not surprisingly, they let you know how you think and feel about 'stuff'. Yes, I know you will say that you know people who say they never dream and I know such people as well. These people are either very well adjusted or have very poor memories. For the rest of us, dreams show us what we are worrying about, but they do it in the language of symbols because this is how your subconscious thinks.

So, for example, if you are worried about the debts you have taken on you might dream about drowning, the link being obvious. Dream diaries and dream interpretation dictionaries can help a lot with this process. A dream diary is something you keep by your bedside and write in (or record on) the moment you wake up after having a dream. If you are like me, then a dream diary isn't a lot of use because when I wake up I'm like a zombie until I've had several cups of tea. It is important, however, to write your dream down as soon as possible because we have all had the situation where we wake up and the dream is extremely vivid, so we are sure that we will remember every detail. Half an hour later we can't remember any of the dream, so it is lost forever.

Dream interpretation dictionaries are also very useful if your symbolism is common. In many years of tutoring Ovates I have rarely found one whose symbolism is completely different. Of course my advice to those particular people is completely wrong and sometimes spectacularly so! Unfortunately the bounds of secrecy do not permit me to elaborate on these, so you will just have to take my word for it. The simplest way to find out if you are one of these people is to write down or recall a recent dream and consult a dream dictionary to see what the symbols mean. If it makes no sense at all, congratulations – you are one of these people! There are many dream dictionaries out there both in print and on the internet, one good one is *Cloud Nine: A Dreamer's Dictionary* by Sandra A Thomson, which also includes some dreamercises to sharpen your skills, which I like because it is quirky. Because of the availability of these dictionaries, I am not going to go into great detail here, but some of the commonest symbols are:

- Being chased means something or someone is pursuing you
- Falling, which shows a fear of letting go
- Nudity, which is showing off yourself to others, may express a desire to be open
- Roads are literally the path that you are following in life
- Houses represent the parts of the mind and different things may be expressed in different rooms
- Being trapped shows a feeling of making the wrong choice or being unable to escape your present life
- Calm pools of water represent peace of mind
- Stormy seas reflect inner turmoil

I guess you get the picture.

Often, as I said earlier, the reason we don't succeed in tasks that we set ourselves is because our subconscious is pulling in a different direction from our conscious mind. This is where dreams score because our subconscious takes control and we can't lie to ourselves any more in a dream. So if in your dreams you find that you are expressing different urges to those that you do consciously then you will know if this applies to you and you can take steps to get your two consciousnesses working together. If you do this you will have passed the Ovate experience and will now be a whole integrated person. Of course if you have frequent terrifying dreams, then there is something wrong and you ought to seek professional help. I am not a psychologist so my advice here is only for those who don't really have any serious problems, which from experience I know is most of us. If you do have serious problems then you will need proper help to sort them out and I would encourage you to seek it.

At this point we naturally come to lucid dreaming. Lucid dreaming is where you retain enough consciousness to steer your dreams rather than being driven by them. Again, I've never found this of much use to me because I feel like I've been travelling all night and am exhausted in the morning. However, like most things, some people swear by this and if it works for them then great and if it works for you then also great.

1) Do you have dreams?
2) Can you interpret them?
3) Is there a message or action that is suggested by your dreams?

Divination

Divination causes a lot of confusion, associated as it is with the occult. However, it need not be so. Divination in the simplest sense means 'to foresee or to be inspired by a God(dess)'. I would argue that the God or Goddess that you want to be inspired by here is yourself. If this sounds a bit arrogant, remember that we (ourselves) are really all that we know and can really influence in this world, so take the leap and inspire yourself. If we use this definition, divination just becomes a way of finding out what we want to do and getting on and doing it. This illustrates nicely divination's importance in Ovate studies; it is the means by which we put our new selves into operation. I know lots of people who divine with tarot cards, runes, omens and so on, and if we are honest with ourselves we all use omens in our daily lives. The commonest one in the UK is probably magpies. There is a rhyme that starts, 'One for sorrow, two for joy,' and many people don't like seeing one magpie as a consequence. In my case the magpie is my totem so I actually enjoy seeing them, the special flash of blue on their backs is particularly inspiring.

In a lot of cases, we don't consciously believe in these superstitions (note the separation between conscious and subconscious again!) but feel that something bad is going to happen when we see one. Ladders are also a very common one. I have watched people go out of their way to avoid passing under a ladder in the street, but this may also have a good deal of common sense here as you can't get a pot of paint dumped on your head if you don't go under the ladder. Nevertheless many people have this superstition.

There is a big difference between mild superstition and obsessive compulsive disorder (or OCD). OCD is where you absolutely have to do things in a certain way otherwise something bad is going to happen and for people with this illness it can be totally paralysing. I knew a colleague once who had to sort his crisps into six neat piles every lunchtime, clearly this is not healthy. The problem, however, is pointing this out in a way that the sufferer can accept. Mostly we just observe in an embarrassed way and carry on with our lives. If you suffer from OCD you will need professional help, so again this advice is for the normally superstitious people among us.

This is an excuse for me to get on my high horse again (another expression meaning to start talking angrily about something bad that someone else has done as if you feel you are better or more clever than they are, which neatly puts me in my place!) as we have touched on the subject of obsession. I have noticed that obsession (certainly in the UK) is growing at an alarming rate in society.

By obsession I mean people becoming unable or unwilling to give things up. Obsession is a need to control that is externalised as the only thing that we can really ever control is ourselves. As a trivial example of obsession, in our block of flats everyone has an assigned parking space at the back, but in the front there are several spaces for visitors. The space in front of our flat is the nearest to the block and people who have perfectly good parking spaces at the back compete to park their cars in this space and get upset when they can't get it. Even when they are denying perfectly legitimate visitors a parking space, they still compete for this space. Are they congenitally lazy or are they just obsessed? I don't think it can be laziness because they have to do more walking with this obsession than they would just walking to their own parking space, because this obsession even requires them to leave their nice cosy warm flats to check if the space is being used and move their cars if it is not. As I said this is a trivial example, but there are many others.

I put it down to the massive sense of entitlement that people in the UK have these days. I blame the parents and socialism in equal measure because parents have given their offspring whatever they wanted, so naturally they expect everything and, as I mentioned earlier, in the socialist conditioning that we grew up in, we expect the state to give us things without having to make the effort ourselves. I know this was not the concept that socialism was meant to inculcate, but it has become an unfortunate side effect.

Another example is Sunday shopping. Sunday has become the biggest shopping day in Guildford because there are no traffic wardens on duty on Sundays. This means that people can just park wherever they like for free. So these are people going out to spend hundreds of pounds on shopping who won't pay a couple of pounds for parking their car. They also tend to park on both sides of the road nearest the high street causing people to have to dodge in and out of gaps to travel down the road. They seem to have no concept that their own cars might get damaged by parking in a dangerous spot, it only matters that they want to park wherever they want.

Anyway enough of the rant, let's get back to divination and in that context let's talk about astrology. Do you have to believe that your path in life is set by the pattern of the stars at your time of birth? No, you don't, but it works equally well either way. I know I will be upsetting many professional astrologers here, but they would agree with me that astrology is not predestination. I find astrology very useful for getting a handle on how you work. Once you are presented with a star chart and its interpretation, you can start arguing with it and say that is like me or that is not. Often perusing a chart will raise things that you have never thought about, and that is divination. It provides a language for you to discuss what motivates you and that is exactly the role of the Ovate. Of course, if you do believe in astrology it is also a lot of fun, thinking about the balance of the elements in your chart, etc.

My own chart, which I had done about 20 years ago, said that I would have a big influence on a spiritual cause in my mid-50s, which I thought was rubbish then as I am a scientist and had no truck with spiritual matters…or so I thought. It is debatable whether knowing that information influenced me in my path in life or not, but as with much in life the scientific control where I didn't do this is not available, so I will never know. In science we call this the Heisenberg uncertainty principle, which means that you can't observe anything without changing it. In fact I am much happier being everyone's best known scientific pagan, so here is an example of divination in practice.

Incidentally, my own chart is astonishingly accurate; I am a Leo with a Gemini ascendant and if you know what this means then it describes me very well. I am happy, fun-loving, prone to having a mane of unruly hair (except when I want to look respectable) and a gifted communicator who loves ideas and stories. On the down side, Leos are the children of the Zodiac, so I am incredibly naïve about people, tending to see the best in everyone and if you want someone to fix your house or car don't call me! (Someone else should do that). I once went to a talk by the English poet Roger McGough; he was talking about funerals and said that he didn't want dignified sadness at his funeral, he wanted distraught women throwing themselves on the coffin! I mentioned to my wife that this sounded like a great idea and she retorted somewhat acidly that it would happen for me!

Despite this, I have Venus in Virgo, so am shy and reticent when it comes to matters of love, but if I give my heart I do completely. Of course overlaid on this is my cultural heritage that we talked about earlier. The Irish tend to have the black dog of depression lurking at their shoulders and have the ability to bear grudges. I do too, but as there is very little earth in my chart I am rather shallow and don't feel things deeply or for long, so I really have to concentrate on the grudge aspect to keep it going.

There are numerous websites that will give you a free chart, providing you know both the time and place of your birth. You also need to know your actual birthday, but most people do know this one. There are also a wealth of books on astrology, so you can make it as much or as little of a study as you wish. I can recommend the aptly named *Astrology for Dummies* by Rae Orion, which provides a simple insight into this subject.

Other methods of divination work equally well, as they all rely on casting some sort of pattern and then using your (or someone else's) insight to interpret the pattern and work out what it means. There will never be a situation where the pattern will unequivocally tell you what it means, they are all open to interpretation. So whether the person doing the reading is actually psychic or just good at reading the little signs by which we all reveal things about ourselves, doesn't matter. You can still get information about yourself that you can use, ponder and come to a conclusion on.

People love using tarot cards and other divination devices, so how about specifically Druidic ways of divination? Let's get away from the historical methods. These were reported by the Romans, who may have not been especially friendly to their subject and would not be practised now, for example stabbing someone in the belly and divining the future from their death throes. That goes by another name these days and carries the appropriate punishment. Also the ritual slaughter of animals and birds is frowned upon and apart from being immoral is probably also very expensive and messy. The ancient Druids also had more benign methods, such as watching the flight of birds, which I have to admit is difficult to get anything from, but is jolly relaxing to watch. The most popular Druidic method these days is the ogham. Ogham is like a secret alphabet, which may have been used to pass secret messages. Of course in a society where most of the people couldn't read, ordinary writing would have served the same objective.

There is some evidence that the Druids used the ogham as a mnemonic to remember things and the most famous of these is the tree ogham. Here each letter of the ogham alphabet is associated with a particular tree. The easiest way to deal with ogham is to download a free ogham font for your word processing program, such as the Celtic ogham font from **www.fontspace.com/curtis-clark/celtic-ogham** and just type in it, ⊤⊞ ⊞ this. The reason you can see the English K in the previous typing is that there isn't a K in Ogham or a J or VWX. If you do it like this you can always highlight the ogham type and use the magic of Word to translate it to English by selecting a readable font. So in case you wanted to know the ogham alphabet is:

English	Ogham	English	Ogham
A	+	N	⊤⊤⊤
B	⊤	O	⊹
C	⊥⊥⊥	P	⊬
D	⊥⊥	Q	⊥⊥⊥⊥
E	⊞	R	⊬⊬
F	⊤⊤	S	⊤⊤⊤
G	⊬	T	⊥⊥
H	⊥	U	⊞
I	⊞⊞	Y	⊬
L	⊤⊤	Z	⊬⊬
M	✗		

Of course you can now exchange secret messages with friends who also have the font because the printed messages will be unreadable by those that haven't. Incidentally this doesn't work in Word because if it doesn't have the font it uses something else anyway! The Ogham letters were designed for carving on stone, wood and metal so they are simple and angular, but were originally not used for English words, hence the missing letters and original inscriptions are thereby difficult to translate as they are not in English. The sharp eyed among you will have noted that they divide into groups based on direction and the number of scratches in the letter. The right scratches; ⊥ ⊥ ⊥ ⊥ ⊥ or H, D, T, C, Q, the left scratches ⊤ ⊤ ⊤ ⊤ ⊤ or B, L, F, S, N, the double scratches, ＋ ＋ ＋ ＋ ＋ or A, O, U, E, I and the sideways scratches, ⧺ ⧺ ⧺ ⧺ ⧺ or M, G, Y, Z, R, and the one that is left, i.e. ⧣, P is the same as Y. The reason that P is on its own is that proto-Celtic originally didn't have a P, until words were borrowed from Latin like Patrick (sic!). Anyway this gives four groups of five letters, which allows you to remember things in groups of five. The most well known of these mnemonic schemes is the tree ogham, where each letter is given the name of a tree (in Celtic of course). So the B group becomes, Beith, Luis, Fearn, Saile and Nuin, which are Birch, Rowan, Alder, Willow and Ash. The H group is Huath, Duir, Tinne, Coll and Quert or in English Hawthorn, Oak, Holly, Hazel and Apple. The vowels are Alim, Onn, Úr, Eadadh and Iodhadh, which are Pine, gorse, heather, Aspen and Yew. The final group are Muin, Gort, Ngetal, Straif and Ruis, or vine, ivy, reed, Blackthorn and Elder. The capital letters for the trees are deliberate here because it makes it obvious that not all of the tree ogham are actually trees.

The first two groups are fine, but the other two are somewhat dubious, so the phrase 'lost in translation' might be appropriate here. There are loads of books and writings devoted to the tree ogham and few notice this simple point. It doesn't matter, however, because what is needed for a divination system is a model that you can generate randomly with sufficient associations to mean something to you. Hence in the tree ogham, we associate each of the trees with a property or quality that gives us something (or rather gives our subconscious something) to work on when we see it. You probably already know that when you are grappling with a difficult problem it goes round and round in your head and often gets nowhere. A divination system allows you to step outside of this non-productive routine and look at your problem from a different perspective. The associations with trees are simple:

- **Birch** is a tree of new beginnings, a nurse tree
- **Rowan** is associated with protection from magic spells, etc
- **Alder** is the quiver tree, constantly in motion
- **Willow** is associated with water and hence emotions and feelings
- **Ash** is the world tree and used for spears, so implies connection
- **Hawthorn** is the May flower and the haws have strong heart stimulatory activity
- **Oak** is the tree of the Druid and also means door
- **Holly** is prickly and also has red berries at Yule
- **Hazel** has nice nuts and is at the Well of Sagais in Celtic mythology, so is associated with wisdom and creativity
- **Apple** has nice fruit and keeps the doctor away, so is associated with health
- **Pine** is the wood of cheap furniture and resin, a clearing smell. It is associated with clarity
- **Broom/gorse** has strong smelling yellow flowers and is the wedding posy of country girls, so is associated with love
- **Heather** is associated with luck, the white kind anyway
- **Aspen** grows very quickly and implies growth
- **Yew** is the tree of death and means the end of something (not necessarily you!)
- **Vine** is the source of wine and coils around things, so implies relaxation
- **Ivy** is a persistent climber, so is associated with determination
- **Reed** is obvious, it bends, so implies flexibility
- **Blackthorn** has the earliest flowers, before the hawthorn, so signifies discipline and getting through a crisis (like winter)
- **Elder** is the tree that you mustn't cut down because it will

44

lead to bad luck (ask DeLorean about his car factory in Northern Ireland!). It is associated with the faeries in mythology and makes excellent drinks. Hence it is associated with renewal and rebirth.

There are many ways to use this system for divination, the easiest is to mark the oghams on identical pieces of card and draw one when you feel in need of insight. You can make more professional sets by using a pyrograph to mark the oghams on pieces of wood or even on twigs gathered from each of the respective trees. This isn't completely possible because some don't have any wood, but use your imagination. Just going through the ritual of formalising your problem and giving yourself space to think about it can help a great deal and the ogham can help you reach the elusive answer. Bear in mind, of course, that divination is not predestination, so if you don't like the answer that you get, you are perfectly at liberty to ignore it or draw again. Like all systems the proof of the pudding is in the eating, meaning if it helps then great. Of course you don't even to have seen a particular tree to do this in an urban environment, it works anywhere, but in a proper Druid course we would go out and find each of the tree oghams and spend some time attuning to it and getting to know it.

1) Do you find divination acceptable or useful?
2) What method(s) do you want to use?
3) Can you get insight into yourself with it?

Gods and Goddesses

Interacting with the Gods and Goddesses is what makes a pagan a pagan (in fact it's the definition of one!) and can be done as easily in an urban environment as in a beautiful waterfall-filled glade. In fact I would argue that it is easier in an urban environment because all you have to do is watch films and read books! What I mean by this is interacting with the archetypes that we call Gods and Goddesses, because as a brief survey of mythology will show you, actually interacting with Gods and Goddesses is often not of great benefit to the mortals involved. The Gods of mythology are rather capricious and don't have the best interests of their worshippers in mind. In fact a main requirement of interacting with a God or Goddess is a great deal of awe and fear. Naturally in our enlightened modern age we don't do a lot of fear and awe (unless you work in a company these days when the annual appraisal is a good cause for a great deal of fear even if awe is not an emotion normally generated).

As always, someone has written the definitive book(s) already and they are called *Gods in Everyman* and *Goddesses in Everywoman* by Jean Shinoda Bolen. This is deity work for the Urban Druid where she has realised that these beings represent deep archetypes of the soul and that we can access them to help us achieve things and become a more well-rounded person. Incidentally, this is a controversial point for some pagans, as interacting with a God or Goddess that they believe in is what motivates them, so if you have this belief then I am not requiring you to believe in my interpretation here, it is entirely up to you.

Also, if you think I have dodged the whole issue of Gods and Goddesses I haven't really because if we look at ancient Egypt, the priests and priestesses who donned the animal masks to become Isis or Horus or so on actually believed that they had become them for the duration of the ceremony, meaning they were just better at it than us. The worshippers were programmed to believe that they were the actual manifestations of the deities because that was their culture and belief system (sorry to land that one on you again!) and their projections of this belief helped the people with the masks to actually believe that they were. This is called positive feedback in science.

We do a similar thing these days with celebrity culture where our projections can be extremely harmful to those celebrities that we project upon. This is most common with celebrities that we project the archetype of Venus, the Goddess of Love, on. Often they can't cope with the intense projections that we are giving them and become self-destructive because people are not deities and shouldn't be. Films and books speak to us when they embody archetypes and we respond to seeing them or reading about them. In fact I would go so far as to say that if there are no archetypal elements in a film or book we find them flat, dull and uninteresting – think about it.

Anyway there are several archetypes deeply written in to our souls and these include the King, the Warrior, the Magician, the Sage, the Trickster, the Healer, the Lover and, for women, the Queen, the Lover, the Mother and more and more often these days the Warrior. The ancient Greeks had this nicely sorted, as you would expect, with their 12 Gods that covered all the archetypes and they hadn't even heard of Jungian analysis in those days! Strictly speaking these aren't archetypes, but expressions of archetypes. However, for the purposes of this book, let's take them as such, otherwise we are into a deep treatise on Jungian psychology, which is beyond me.

The main idea of this concept is that you can identify which of the deities you are naturally drawn to and learn how to express the others (in the correct balance of course) in your life. If you need to express authority then Zeus is your deity or if you need to stand up for something then Ares (the God of War) will help. Of great interest to Druids is the Magician archetype, because magicians are adept at transforming energy or to put it a bit simpler, changing their behaviour to overcome bad habits. So this archetype is one that everyone needs to express and come to terms with. The Sage means what it says; a sage is a fount of knowledge, so when you need access to your memory you need this one.

The Trickster is found in many pantheons; probably the most familiar would be the Raven in the Native American mythos and Loki in the Norse. The Trickster is obviously a necessary archetype as the Norse Gods never did away with Loki, no matter what he did. They got fed up and chained him up in the end, but he survived. The Trickster also corresponds to the Shadow and more than anything else the Ovate experience involves owning this. We all have a Shadow, the sum of the bad and ignoble things that we have done, but we mostly ignore it and hope that, whatever we have done, it won't happen again. This is putting one's head into the sand, as we really ought to acknowledge that we are all capable of doing bad things. We need to realise that potential in ourselves and then strive to do good instead. We can forgive ourselves when we fail, but we must seek to do good. The Trickster doesn't take things seriously and finds alternative ways of doing things, often unconventionally, and we all need to do this from time to time.

The Healer is obvious, as we all need healing or to give healing at some time. There is always a God or Goddess of Love, as this is an archetype that we really ought to express in our daily lives and often don't. I had a Freudian slip when I was typing that last sentence and typed daily loves instead, which is actually more appropriate. This God or Goddess also expresses the destructive aspect of love, as failing in love or loving the wrong person can really destroy us. However, the happier side, where we find someone to love who really loves you back, is the highest experience that we can have in this life. I can't speak for experiences in the other lives (if any) as I haven't got there yet!

When, you might ask in a book about Druidry, is he going to get to Celtic deities? Here we find a problem as the Celts seemed to have an enormous pantheon of deities, sometimes associated with streams, rivers and so forth, who we would now call spirits of place and even more confusingly they all had local names. The classic example of this is the Goddess of the sacred spring at Bath, who is known as Sulis. The Romans, being sensible people, realised that this problem existed and conflated the local deities with the nearest equivalent of their own (who were borrowed more or less wholesale from the Greeks anyway!). Sulis was identified with Minerva, the Goddess of Wisdom (Athena in the Greek mythos), so represents the Sage aspect of the female psyche (among other attributes). So getting a handle on the Celtic deities is like juggling with fish, they keep slipping out of your hands! In order to make things simple I am going to choose the deities that fit my argument and am telling you this up front so that there will be no confusion. Often in New Age work, the prejudice of the author is presented as fact without reference, so at least you know what I'm doing here.

The Dagda corresponds to the King archetype, being the leader of the mythical Tuatha de Danann, the magical people who inhabited Ireland before the Milesians came and conquered them. He is often depicted as carrying a club and possessing a huge cauldron. As he was probably a God of the Earth and Sky, the image of an inverted cauldron as the bowl of the sky fits here. As King, the club relates to the King's role in dispensing justice. He has two brothers, Ogma and Lir, Ogma being the Sage and Lir the God of the Sea, so therefore representing the flow of the emotions. I quite like this rendering with the King being supported by his heart (Lir) and his head (Ogma). Now where have we seen that before? That's right Star Trek. Captain Kirk (the King) travels the universe, advised by his head and heart in the characters of Mr Spock and Dr McCoy. So you can learn a lot about this by just watching old TV series, which is just about as urban as you can get!

Strangely enough it is easier to find a female Celtic Warrior Goddess than a male God and she is probably the most well-known Celtic deity. I don't know if this says something about Celtic women? Anyway the best male Celtic War God is Toutates, who is familiar to anyone who has read the Asterix the Gaul comics, where they use the phrase, 'By Toutatis!' There are actually several inscriptions known that refer to Toutatis and he is even mentioned by the Roman writer Lucan, so compared to the others he is relatively well documented. Unfortunately there are few if any descriptions of him and no stories that I know. He is also not part of the Tuatha de Danann, but was clearly known and worshipped and has been associated with the Roman God Mars, who was the God of War. Urban Warrior archetypes abound, just watch any adventure film or read a James Bond novel. The interesting thing about them is their lack of character, it seems that anything that detracts from the clear Warrior archetype makes for a poorer story. My favourite quote is from Christopher Paolini, who wrote the Eragon stories. He said, 'The hero, who let's face it isn't very bright...' To reiterate, the Warrior archetype doesn't just relate to fighting and killing, it relates to situations where courage is called for and you need to stand up for yourself and be confident, like in your annual appraisal if you have one.

The Magician archetype is also difficult to pin down, but the best candidates are Amergin and Taliesin, who incidentally share some of the same stories. Amergin was the leader of the Milesians who invaded Ireland and defeated the Tuatha de Danann. Amergin romantically named the island after his new bride, the Queen of the Tuatha de Danann, who was called Eriu. Amergin is famed for singing a magic song that enabled the invading Milesians to land when they were held back by the Druids of the Tuatha de Danann who had conjured up a storm. The Urban Magician has to be Merlin, who is famed for his magical lore and may even be an actual Druid in some readings of his story.

The Celtic Mercury, associated with thieves and trickery, among other things, is traditionally Lugus (or Lugh). Lugus was skilled in all of the arts like Mercury and carried a spear that would strike by itself and was always hungry for blood. This can be equated with the flash of divine inspiration, which is how Tricksters overcome their enemies. He appears to either have been or became the chief God of the Celts, his aspect as Lugh of the Long Hand linking him with being a Sun God, the long hand being the rays of the sun. On an urban level, the most well-known Trickster is probably B'rer Rabbit, who uses his wits to overcome his enemies.

The most famous Celtic Healer has to be the Tuatha de Danann's physician Diancecht, who is best known for his jealousy. He killed his son in a fit of jealousy because he could make a working arm of flesh and blood and Diancecht couldn't. When his daughter Airmed wept over the grave of her brother, all the healing herbs in the world grew. Airmed carefully catalogued the uses of all of these herbs, but Diancecht mixed them all up so that the knowledge would not become generally available. This clearly represents the secret knowledge of physicians, which gives them their status over everyone else. Urban mythology abounds with the Healer, just watch any hospital programme on the television currently or, if you are a little older like myself, think of Dr Kildare or Dr Finlay. Incidentally, this aspect of healing and the emotions is strongly emphasised with the story of Diancecht, but also with Dr McCoy in Star Trek.

Finally, we get to the Lover, a powerful archetype and surprisingly enough there is a male Celtic candidate. This is Aengus, who is sometimes described as having singing birds circling his head. Interestingly he owned a sword called 'the Great Fury', which is pretty obvious to those who have been crossed in love and was said to be able to breathe life back into broken bodies, which is again obvious. There are numerous examples of the

Urban Lover, James Bond being one and new instances arise all of the time, so you don't have to search hard.

As I said before it is easier to get an acceptable set of Goddess archetypes from the Celtic mythos. It is easy to understand that patriarchy may have been a later development when you look at Celtic deities because you may have struggled with the male ones given earlier, but you will probably already know most of the female Celtic deities.

The Queen can be the before mentioned Eriu, whose name means either the land or fat (!), depending on which sources you read. I guess that the fat here refers to the fertility and beauty of the land. The other candidate is Danu, who is the Mother Goddess of the Tuatha de Danann and therefore Queen of them all. Her name may remain in Danube, so she may have been a river Goddess and not a land Goddess, but this is another indication of the reverence the Celts had for rivers. In the UK they tossed objects into rivers and lakes, presumably as offerings to the God or Goddess resident there. Some of these objects were extremely valuable and included ornate swords and shields, which were the equivalent of heaving your new Porsche car into the lake!

Unfortunately, there are no stories about Danu, at least not any I could find easily, but the aspect of the Queen is easily understood. One aspect of this that stands out in Celtic mythology is her aspect as conferring sovereignty over the land. To be the consort of the Queen gives you the right to rule, but if you abuse her you forfeit this right like Arthur and Guinevere in the Arthurian mythos. I am conflating Queen and Mother here because everyone knows that mothers rule the roost. The most well known example of the Queen archetype is Queen Elizabeth I of England, who inspired the growth of England into a world power with the cult of Gloriana. However, finding positive urban interpretations of the Queen archetype is actually quite difficult. In the cult Game of Thrones TV series, Queen Cersei is actually not a very nice person, but the younger Queen Margaery is (or seems to be anyway). I put this down to the fact that George R. R. Martin prefers to write about grey characters rather than invalidating my precept.

The Warrior Goddess is best known as the Morrigan, the Triple Goddess of the Celts. The name either means great queen or nightmare/phantom queen, clearly flagging up the horror of war. She has three aspects, the other two being Badb and Macha. Badb appears as a hooded crow whose flight over battlefields spreads fear and confusion. Macha, which seems to mean 'a plain', is somewhat confusing until you learn that the crop of Macha is the severed heads of the men who have died in battle. As I mentioned earlier this archetype seems to have become emphasised in recent years with the growing interest in martial arts among women and numerous urban examples like Buffy the Vampire Slayer, Xena the Warrior Princess, etc. The strong aspect of the Warrior Woman in Celtic culture is emphasised by Scathach who trains Cucullain (the archetypal Irish Male Warrior) in the arts of war! Interestingly Cucullain was chosen to represent both the struggle for a united Ireland and the hopes of the loyalists, having been associated with what is now Northern Ireland.

Epona was the Celtic Horse Goddess and was also associated with grain, so presumably with fertility. Epona was also the only Celtic deity to be worshipped in Rome, presumably because there wasn't a Roman equivalent! The link between women and horses is still a strong one today and relates to the female way of acting in partnership with something rather than dominating it (men often prefer cars or motorbikes, but this is a generalisation so there are women who prefer cars and motorbikes and men who like to act in partnership!). Epona may also have been a psychopomp, a guide of the dead, which raises the delightful image of the souls of the dead riding off on white horses (the Norse already have this association with the Valkyries). There is also some support for the idea that the apparent taboo about eating horse meat in the UK may be a remnant of the worship of Epona. There are again countless examples of this archetype in the urban world, ask any young girl in her horse phase. There are numerous books and films celebrating this, one need only think of *Black Beauty*, Flambards and Follyfoot.

The Goddess of Healing is Brigit, who is known for healing, smithcraft and fire and may be the St Brigit of Kildare who is worshipped by nuns tending an eternal flame today. This archetype relates to elevated states and purity, the raising of the soul for healing, the raising of the bronze to new forms in smithcraft and the rush of fire. She is also known as the patron Goddess of the Druids, because as Druids we seek that fire of inspiration and healing in our daily lives, so definitely an archetype to concentrate on. She embodies the Roman Minerva and Greek Athena, the knowledgeable Warrior Woman. The female Healer is best known to us as Florence Nightingale in the Crimean war, the lady with the lamp. She is also familiar to us as the nurse in hospital dramas, which in the past represented the downgrading of the female Healer role, but thankfully nowadays there are female doctors in these programmes as well. The 1990s TV series Dr. Quinn, Medicine Woman was a pioneer in this respect, especially as she was a female doctor in a time when it was virtually unheard of.

Aine is the Celtic Goddess of Love, also known as the Queen of the Fairies. Again she is no shrinking violet as one of the stories about her relates her biting off the ear of a man who raped her, thereby under old Irish law making him unfit to be a king, as kings had to be whole and unblemished. So treat love with respect, as if you didn't know that already. Unfortunately there seems to be a lot of rape in the old Irish stories, but they were recorded a long time ago. She is also associated with Midsummer, to many the perfect time for love. The Lover is an aspect that is ubiquitous in the media, every so called 'chick flick' is about this and in fact almost every book or film ever made. I could list examples of this urban archetype all day, but maybe Scarlett Johansson merits a mention here as the enigmatic black widow in the Avengers film series.

Unfortunately I struggled with a Celtic Goddess of Magic, who would have been reduced in status and called a witch in the past. Magicians were seen as noble and searching for hidden truths whereas witches were just plain evil. Fortunately this perception has changed and the epithet witch is now not an insulting one. I thought I'd better get that one in, as a lot of my fellow Moon Books authors are witches and jolly nice people they are too! The reason I struggled is that all women are magical to some extent and this is especially true of Celtic mythology where most of the Goddesses expressed some magical prowess. The best candidate I can come up with is Ceridwen, the Crone Goddess who stirs a magical cauldron of inspiration from which Taliesin manages to steal three drops of inspiration. She is Goddess of the Moon, which is often associated with the magical side of women. She chases Taliesin in a series of transformations into animals, birds and fish and can't be that much of a crone as she rebirths Taliesin after eating him when he is disguised as a grain of corn and she is transformed into a hen. This has all the aspects we are looking for, inspiration and transformation, the tasks of the Magician archetype. It is also interesting that the arts of war were taught by women as well as the arts of magic, as the story above is clearly an initiation rite. Finding a positive aspect of the female Magician was difficult in past culture, but this is changing rapidly and one has only to think of Marion Zimmer Bradley's *Mists of Avalon* series, which stands out in this respect and more recently Sonea in Trudi Canavan's *Black Magician* series and, of course, the supremely intelligent witch Hermione Granger in *Harry Potter*.

The Sage has arisen as a contemporary archetype for women with the sexy computer nerd Felicity Smoke in the TV series

Arrow and the genius Clara Oswald in Doctor Who, which is very encouraging and long may it continue. The Celtic Goddess mostly associated with this trait is Brigit, but as I mentioned earlier Sulis also has a claim as the Romans associated her with Minerva, their Goddess of Wisdom.

Many pagans invoke the Gods and Goddesses by actually praying to them, which is a good way to ponder on their qualities and absorb them. If you want to know about Druid prayer, I heartily recommend Joanna Van der Hoeven's book *The Awen Alone*, which has a good section on praying. If you are not the praying type then the same effect can be achieved by studying the archetypes, working out what qualities they have that you would like in your own life and then trying to express these qualities in your everyday actions. If you can manage to integrate all of the essential qualities in a balanced way then congratulations, you are a whole human being and you don't need to do any more work on yourself.

In practice, most of us never achieve this and have to keep going back and reminding ourselves of how we should have acted in that situation and trying to do it properly next time. This can be a monotonously repetitive process, but keep at it and it does get easier believe me!

1) Think of the 12 God and Goddess archetypes that you want to explore.
2) Think about the qualities that they embody.
3) Research them by watching films with these archetypes in them or reading books.
4) If you are in a situation where, for example, the Trickster is called for, think about how the Trickster would deal with it.
5) If it helps, carry out the identified action.

Fith Fath or Shape Shifting

Many Ovates like to experience other forms of life by doing what is called fith fath or, as it is more commonly known, shape shifting. Many believe that they actually do change shape, but it really doesn't matter if you do or not because if you are doing this sitting on your own urban sofa and you are still there afterwards then it makes no difference. If you have read *The Once and Future King* series by T. H. White you will be familiar with this and also if you have watched the Disney Sword in the Stone cartoon (which is based on the books). In these the young King Arthur is transformed into a number of birds and animals by Merlin, so that he can learn the lessons of kingship. So this is the point, to use this experience to understand something about the animals concerned that you can then bring into your own life. It requires a fair deal of imagination (which is why the imagination is trained in the Bardic grade first), as you have to think about how the animal moves, senses things, and so on, but it can be a great deal of fun and a great stress reliever. This bit comes after the Gods and Goddesses bit because it is essentially the same thing, we associate qualities with animals and birds that are useful to us and seek to enhance these in our own beings. For example, hawks are associated with keen sight, so if you feel you need to see something clearly concentrating on Hawk will help. Everyone has different associations with particular birds and animals but here is a useful and short list:

Tigers are associated with ferocity and strength
Wolves with determination and being part of a pack
Boars with tenacity and ferocity
Cats with grace and self sufficiency
Dogs with loyalty
Horses with speed and fluidity

Lions with courage and rulership

Foxes with cunning

Owls with wisdom and seeing through the darkness

Spiders with fate and destiny

Swans were sacred to the Celts because they embodied all four elements, Air, Earth, Water and Fire (because they hiss like a dragon!), so represent togetherness. So this is a great totem to have and you would be lucky to get it.

There is a ritual in the Ovate course where the student gains their totem animal. I always know if they have done it properly because of the surprise they evidence, the more unusual and surprising the animal the better. Everyone wants Wolf or Lion, but usually gets something else that has a lesson for them. A friend once complained angrily that she had got a cartoon chipmunk as a totem, but Chipmunk is associated with abundance, nurturing, the sense of hearing and travel. So it is a pretty good totem to have and also teaches us not to take things at face value. In case you were wondering or paying attention earlier, Magpie is associated with omens and prophecies. Magpies appear pretty much and black and white, but if you watch carefully you will see the secret flash of blue. They also like to collect pretty baubles and shiny objects, so these are all worth pondering on. I know they have some unpleasant habits as well but doesn't everyone! If you would like to know a bit more about fith fath then I would recommend *Druidry and Meditation* by Nimue Brown, which deals with this nicely.

1) What animal or bird comes to mind when you allow yourself to think of one, without determining it?
2) What qualities would you associate with this animal or bird?
3) Do you need to express these qualities more in your daily life?

Putting it Together

Right, now we come to the crunch moment. If you have followed this far, has it helped? In a proper Druid course you would spend a lot of time doing guided meditations and rituals to uncover the aspects discussed in this book and change your responses to the ones that are no longer appropriate. However, this can be dangerous without proper support and guidance so I'm not going to go into this here. If you are interested you know what to do! However, if you have only become aware of what makes you do what you do then you have won half of the battle already. A colleague of mine used to say that her copy of M. Scott Peck's *The Path Less Travelled* would fall open at the right places as she had used it so often, but she just couldn't do what she ought to do. She was actually one of the most spiritual people I have met, but didn't have the confidence. Remember you always have a choice and no one can make you do things that you don't want to do. Those who feel that they don't have a choice just know that the results of the choice will be unacceptable and in some cases this can be true. However, knowing this and not making the choice is still a choice. The main problem is how much baggage you are carrying around, both emotionally and as a result of conditioning, the more that you have the more work on yourself you will have to do. No one else can do this for you, it is entirely up to you, which is the beauty of spiritual development as you can do it on your own whenever and wherever you like. Hence my concept of Urban Druidry, it is possible to do it anywhere, you are only limited by what your mind and imagination can do. Believe me, it is infinitely better to be in charge of your own life, it is ironically much less stressful because you are being true to yourself. Of course we all fail from time to time, but we wouldn't be human if we didn't. So blessings on the new you:

May the nourishment of the earth be yours,
May the clarity of light be yours,
May the fluency of the ocean be yours,
May the protection of the ancestors be yours.
(www.faithandworship.com/Celtic_Blessings_and_Prayers.ht
m#ixzz3lLZAXIkc)

Reading List

Your Genetic Inheritance
The Seven Daughters of Eve by Bryan Sykes, 2004, Corgi, ISBN: 978-0552152181

Your Local Environment
Pygmalion (Penguin Classics) by George Bernard Shaw, 2003, Penguin, ISBN: 978-0141439501
The House of Doctor Dee by Peter Ackroyd
Dan Leno and the Limehouse Golem by Peter Ackroyd
The Angel of the West Window by Gustav Meyrink, 2010, Dedalus Ltd, ISBN: 978-1903517819
The Golem (European Classics) by Gustav Meyrink, 1995, Dedalus Ltd, ISBN: 978-1873982914

The Pressures of Expectations
Healing the impossible?
There are no Incurable Diseases: Dr. Schulze's 30-Day Cleansing & Detoxification Program by Richard Schulze, 1999, Natural Healing Pubns, ISBN: 978-0967156736

The Ancestors
The problems with the ancestors succinctly explained.
This be the Verse by Philip Larkin in *Philip Larkin Poems: Selected by Martin Amis* by Philip Larkin, 2011, Faber and Faber, ISBN-13: 978-0571258109

Where are you in History?
The Wreck of the Mary Gloster by Rudyard Kipling, www.kiplingsociety.co.uk/poems_gloster.htm

Death

Death clarified.

The Journey into Spirit: A Pagan's Perspective on Death, Dying, and Bereavement by Kristoffer Hughes, 2014, Llewellyn Publications, U.S. ISBN 978-0738740751

The Tibetan Book of the Dead: First Complete Translation (Penguin Classics) by Graham Coleman and Thupten Jinpa, 2006, Penguin, ISBN: 978-0140455298

Healing and Herbalism

Agricola and Germania (Penguin Classics) by Tacitus, 2010, ISBN: 978-0140455403

A Druid's Herbal for the Sacred Earth Year by Ellen Evert Hopman, Destiny Books, 1994, ISBN: 978-0892815012

Love

www.goodreads.com/list/show/550.Best_Love_Stories_

Dreams

How to interpret dreams in an accessible way.

Cloud Nine: A Dreamer's Dictionary by Sandra A. Thomson, 2000, Avon Books, ISBN: 978-0380808892

Divination

A simple overview of astrology for the uninitiated.

Astrology for Dummies by Rae Orion, 2007, John Wiley and Sons Ltd. ISBN: 978-0470098400

Gods and Goddesses

Archetypes of the Gods and Goddesses.

Goddesses in Everywoman: Thirtieth Anniversary Edition: Powerful Archetypes in Women's Lives by Jean Shinoda Bolen, 2014, Harper Paperbacks; ISBN 978-0062321121

Gods in Everyman: Archetypes That Shape Men's Lives by Jean

Shinoda Bolen, 2014, Harper Paperbacks, ISBN 978-0062329943
Practical praying for Druids.
Pagan Portals – The Awen Alone: Walking the Path of the Solitary Druid by Joanna van der Hoeven, 2014, Moon Books, ISBN: 978-1782795476

Fith Fath

Fith fath explained.

Druidry and Meditation by Nimue Brown, 2012, Moon Books, ISBN: 978-1780990286

The Once and Future King by T.H. White, 1996, Harper Voyager, ISBN: 978-0006483014

Moon Books

PAGANISM & SHAMANISM

What is Paganism? A religion, a spirituality, an alternative belief system, nature worship? You can find support for all these definitions (and many more) in dictionaries, encyclopaedias, and text books of religion, but subscribe to any one and the truth will evade you. Above all Paganism is a creative pursuit, an encounter with reality, an exploration of meaning and an expression of the soul. Druids, Heathens, Wiccans and others, all contribute their insights and literary riches to the Pagan tradition. Moon Books invites you to begin or to deepen your own encounter, right here, right now.

If you have enjoyed this book, why not tell other readers by posting a review on your preferred book site. Recent bestsellers from Moon Books are:

Journey to the Dark Goddess
How to Return to Your Soul
Jane Meredith
Discover the powerful secrets of the Dark Goddess and transform your depression, grief and pain into healing and integration.
Paperback: 978-1-84694-677-6 ebook: 978-1-78099-223-5

Shamanic Reiki
Expanded Ways of Working with Universal Life Force Energy
Llyn Roberts, Robert Levy
Shamanism and Reiki are each powerful ways of healing;
together, their power multiplies. *Shamanic Reiki* introduces
techniques to help healers and Reiki practitioners tap ancient
healing wisdom.
Paperback: 978-1-84694-037-8 ebook: 978-1-84694-650-9

Pagan Portals - The Awen Alone
Walking the Path of the Solitary Druid
Joanna van der Hoeven
An introductory guide for the solitary Druid, *The Awen Alone*
will accompany you as you explore, and seek out your own
place within the natural world.
Paperback: 978-1-78279-547-6 ebook: 978-1-78279-546-9

A Kitchen Witch's World of Magical Herbs & Plants
Rachel Patterson
A journey into the magical world of herbs and plants, filled with
magical uses, folklore, history and practical magic. By popular
writer, blogger and kitchen witch, Tansy Firedragon.
Paperback: 978-1-78279-621-3 ebook: 978-1-78279-620-6

Medicine for the Soul
The Complete Book of Shamanic Healing
Ross Heaven
All you will ever need to know about shamanic healing and
how to become your own shaman...
Paperback: 978-1-78099-419-2 ebook: 978-1-78099-420-8

Shaman Pathways - The Druid Shaman
Exploring the Celtic Otherworld
Danu Forest
A practical guide to Celtic shamanism with exercises and
techniques as well as traditional lore for exploring the Celtic
Otherworld.
Paperback: 978-1-78099-615-8 ebook: 978-1-78099-616-5

Traditional Witchcraft for the Woods and Forests
A Witch's Guide to the Woodland with Guided Meditations and
Pathworking
Melusine Draco
A Witch's guide to walking alone in the woods, with guided
meditations and pathworking.
Paperback: 978-1-84694-803-9 ebook: 978-1-84694-804-6

Wild Earth, Wild Soul
A Manual for an Ecstatic Culture
Bill Pfeiffer
Imagine a nature-based culture so alive and so connected,
spreading like wildfire. This book is the first flame...
Paperback: 978-1-78099-187-0 ebook: 978-1-78099-188-7

Naming the Goddess
Trevor Greenfield
Naming the Goddess is written by over eighty adherents and
scholars of Goddess and Goddess Spirituality.
Paperback: 978-1-78279-476-9 ebook: 978-1-78279-475-2

Shapeshifting into Higher Consciousness
Heal and Transform Yourself and Our World with Ancient
Shamanic and Modern Methods
Llyn Roberts
Ancient and modern methods that you can use every day
to transform yourself and make a positive difference in the
world.
Paperback: 978-1-84694-843-5 ebook: 978-1-84694-844-2

Readers of ebooks can buy or view any of these bestsellers
by clicking on the live link in the title. Most titles are published
in paperback and as an ebook. Paperbacks are available in
traditional bookshops. Both print and ebook formats are
available online.

Find more titles and sign up to our readers' newsletter at
http://www.johnhuntpublishing.com/paganism.

Follow us on Facebook at
https://www.facebook.com/MoonBooks
and Twitter at https://twitter.com/MoonBooksJHP.